COPING WITH GRIEF: YOUR HAPPINESS IS IN YOUR HEALING

WRITTEN BY

LYNNETTE M. CLEMENT, ED.M.
ERICA STERLING-BUSH, M.S.

COPING WITH GRIEF: YOUR HAPPINESS IS IN YOUR HEALING

© 2022 by LYNNETTE M. CLEMENT, ED.M. and ERICA STERLING-BUSH, M.S.

Published by: Lulu Press, Inc.

All rights reserved. No part of this book may be reproduced, copied, stored in a retrieval system, or transmitted in any form or means – electronic, mechanical, photocopy, recording, film, song, music, video, or otherwise; without written permission from the authors, except for brief quotations in printed reviews.

Library of Congress Cataloguing in Publication Data
LYNNETTE M. CLEMENT, ED.M.
ERICA STERLING-BUSH, M.S.
  COPING WITH GRIEF: YOUR HAPPINESS IS IN YOUR HEALING by LYNNETTE M. CLEMENT, ED.M. and ERICA STERLING-BUSH, M.S.

Library of Congress Number:
TXu 2-347-871
ISBN: 978-1-387-50776-4

Printed in the United States of America

About the Authors

Lynnette M. Clement is from Philadelphia, PA. She has over 20 years of experience working in higher education, is an author, award winning actress, and entrepreneur. Lynnette earned a Bachelor of Arts in Psychology and a Master of Arts in Education. She is the President and CEO of *Love Exquisite Cosmetics, LLC* dba *Love Exquisite, LLC* and the online *Love Exquisite Magazine*, which is under the umbrella of her publishing company *Love Exquisite Media and Press Publishing, LLC*. She also volunteers as co-host on the internet-based radio show, *Real Recognize Real Talk Radio*. Lynnette is the author of the books, *Ardent Grandeur* and *Cheaters Never Win: How to Stop Cheating in Any Relationship or Never Start*, which are both about making better life decisions and figuring out your "why."

In 2021, Lynnette founded the 501(c)(3) *L.E.A.R.N. Center* with the mission of helping to end senseless gun violence in Philadelphia. Consider donating at www.LearnNpc.org.

Erica Sterling-Bush is the co-author of this book, Coping with Grief: Your Happiness is in Your Healing. She is from Philadelphia, PA and has over 26 years of professional experience focusing on web development, instructional design, and digital marketing. Erica currently works as an Instructional Designer, Educator and Web Strategist. Erica earned a M.S. in Instructional Technology Management from a private 4-year University, and a B.S. in Chemical Engineering and Education from Drexel University. Erica enjoys music, traveling, helping others succeed, and technology. She is the owner of *Websiteplant, LLC*, which is a web design and eLearning company.

Coping with Grief: Your Happiness is in Your Healing
Lynnette M. Clement, Ed.M.
Erica Sterling-Bush, M.S.

Book Cover Designer: Rebecca Covers

Table of Contents

Preface..5

I. What is Grief..............................6

II. Dealing with Depression....................11

III. Don't Take Any Day for Granted.........39

IV. Coping with Grief after the Loss of a Friend..47

V. Coping with Grief after the Loss of a Family Member...................................52

VI. Coping with Grief after the Loss of a Relationship...60

VII. Embracing Change............................66

VIII. How to Help Loved Ones Cope with Grief...70

IX. How to Help a Child Understand Grief and Loss..80

X. Go Through, to Get Through................86

XI. Your Happiness Is In Your Healing.....95

Resources...110

References..112

Preface

After dealing with any type of loss, it is not always easy to find your peace and happiness. However, your happiness is in your healing. Coping with grief requires you to go through the stages of grief to get to your healing. Healing is a process. Give yourself the time you need to heal after a loss; knowing that the time needed to heal is different for everyone. This self-help book, Coping with Grief: Your Happiness is in Your Healing, is written with love, encouragement, and empowerment to give readers the strategies, support, and resources that can help people who are struggling to heal after a loss. When applying the suggested strategies, this self-help book will help readers develop healthy coping skills, understand the grieving process, and be open to working towards healing.

I.   What is Grief?

The Merriam-Webster dictionary defines grief as, "Deep and poignant distress caused by or as if by bereavement; a cause of such suffering; annoying or playful criticism, and an unfortunate outcome." Grief is also defined as deep sorrow, caused by someone's death or a loss. Prolonged grief can lead to depression. Over time, we learn how to deal with grief in a better way. However, our thoughts or reminders about what we lost can trigger feelings of sadness. This sadness can lead to depression if we do not allow ourselves to go *through* the stages of grief properly. Identifying someone who is experiencing grief is different from being able to identify someone who is dealing with depression. For example, a grieving person may pretend to be happy when they are surrounded by friends and family who support them, but a memory of something or someone they lost, can cause them to feel sad in that moment.

However, with depression, people usually prefer to be in isolation and have feelings of sadness beyond that moment of thought about what they lost. Depression is more severe than grief and can lead to thoughts of suicide or other harmful behavior. It is so important to develop better coping skills to go through the stages of grief and find your happiness.

There are different stages of grief. Those stages are:

- **Denial** - As soon as you hear sad news or experience a traumatic event, your response at first can be disbelief. You may be in a state of shock or do not feel anything. The news can feel like a bad dream that you do not want to believe is true.

- **Anger** - After you begin to accept the reality of any tragic event, you might begin to feel upset about what occurred. Your anger could be directed towards those around you. Perhaps, it could be because you are looking for someone to blame for what happened. You might also feel angry at yourself for feeling powerless. Some people get mad at God for allowing the tragic event to occur. If the traumatic event is the death of a parent, you might also be mad at the parent who died, feeling like he/she is leaving you all alone.
- **Bargaining** – Is used as a defense mechanism to try to guard your emotions. You try to convince yourself that you are okay to postpone the hurt and sadness. You replay the events in your head and wonder if there was

something that you could have done to prevent the tragic event from happening.

- **Depression** – Is an emotional state of mind and being. The more you think about your experience as a tragedy and loss, you feel sad. You usually do not want anyone to tell you how to think or feel. It is a prolonged sadness. You cry often, and have **trouble sleeping,** eating, and being around friends and family. Depression often feels like a sense of hopelessness and giving up on the notion that things will get better. If left unacknowledged or untreated, suicidal ideation can result.
- **Acceptance** – You are no longer in denial about what happened. You accept reality and are ready to feel better about what happened. Although, you might still be upset, you are ready to

move on with your life *(Kubler-Ross & Kessler, 2007)*.

Before we help you cope with grief, we want to make sure that you understand what grief is. Everyone goes through the stages of grief. The timeframe in which each person goes through the stages of grief could be different and the order of the stages can vary from person to person as well. It is also possible that after you have gone through the stages of grief, another tragic event could cause you to relive past traumas and you will have to go through the stages again, and that is okay; just do not get stuck at any of the stages. When you do not allow yourself to go through the stages of grief, you can experience prolonged feelings of depression.

II. Dealing with Depression

If you or someone you know has suddenly lost interest in doing the things you/they normally love, have trouble sleeping, or sleep too much, there is a possibility that you are depressed. Sometimes, the symptoms of depression are subtle, and sometimes the symptoms can be obvious. The main things to notice to be able to identify depression are: feelings of hopelessness, being sad over an extended period, and the feelings of emptiness that last more than two weeks. If you experience any of those emotions, you could be suffering from depression. Thankfully, depression is very treatable. If you want to feel better, you might have to get professional help. Getting professional help does not mean that there is something wrong with you. It means that you are having a challenging time dealing with depression on your own.

There are several reasons why some people do not get help when dealing with depression. Usually, the reasons why some people do not get help involve: not having the right insurance, not being able to afford the care, not accepting that you are suffering from depression, or convinced by your friends and family that what you are experiencing is not "that serious" or what you are feeling is "fake." Do not allow the stigma associated with depression or money to stand in your way of getting help. There are people that can help you, regardless of your financial situation. At the end of this book, we provide you with several resources to help you. After you get the help, you need to deal with depression in a better way, you will be glad you did.

If your depressive symptoms have persisted for a lengthy period time, be honest with your doctor about your mental state of mind. If you want to truly get adequate support and help, you must provide full disclosure and be open to the vulnerability of sharing your story, without leaving anything to the imagination. Even if you are not sure if it is related to depression, you must tell the truth and be honest, so that you can be accurately diagnosed and treated. The type of treatment people with depression can receive is based on the type of depressive state they are in.

According to the Diagnostic and Statistical Manual of Mental Disorder (DSM), there are several types of depression. The types of depression are:

- **Major Depression** – Feelings of worthlessness, hopelessness, suicidal thoughts, excessive negative thought, and inappropriate feelings of guilt that you experience every day. Usually there is a combination of symptoms that last for two weeks or longer. Statistics show that major depression affects an estimated twenty-one million adults in the U.S. Sadly, most of the people suffering from depression do not know that what they are experiencing is depression and therefore they do not seek appropriate help. Major depression can be unilateral (an individual who experiences excessive negative emotions that do not change between two mood states) or bipolar (frequent mood changes between depression and mania). These symptoms interfere with your ability to enjoy everyday life.

- **Dysthymia** – Persistent mild depression that lasts for a lengthy period and if it lasts at least two years, it can lead to major depression. It is considered a long-term, "low mood" persistent depressive disorder that is treatable by a medical professional. Some days you are able to be happy, but depression prevents you from staying happy. Dysthymia differs from bipolar; you do not have manic episodes.

- **Bipolar Disorder** – Formerly diagnosed as "manic depressive" episodes of mood swings ranging from depression, low mood to manic high energy (mania or hypomania) mood swings.

- **Seasonal Affective Disorder (SAD)** – Depression that occurs with the changes of the seasons and the weather. It is said that rain and darkness are considered gloomy and therefore some people experience low mood depression and sadness based on those conditions. In fall and winter, the weather is colder, and it usually gets darker earlier, so for those people who prefer hotter weather and daylight, they might experience low mood depression. On the contrary, there are some people who prefer colder weather and, in the spring, and summer seasons they might experience low mood depression as well. Basically, in all situations, their mood changes as the season changes. For people who prefer sunlight, light therapy could be the best treatment.

- **Psychotic Depression** – Severe clinical depression. A person may suffer from delusions, false beliefs that are disturbing to others, and even hear voices and see things that are not there.

- **Postpartum Depression** – Depression that can occur after giving birth to a child. The postpartum period is usually the first four to six weeks after birth; however, it can also occur during pregnancy. Feelings of sadness that is considered, "the baby blues" that last longer than two weeks is considered postpartum depression. Postpartum depression is a hormonal imbalance that can last as long as a woman is breastfeeding. It can interfere with life and the joy of being a parent.

- **Premenstrual Dysphoric Disorder** – Severe form of premenstrual syndrome includes: expressions of anger, being easily irritated, and extreme sadness that occurs at the onset of menstruation that causes extreme mood swings that can impact the ability to work and engage in everyday activities.

- **Situational Depression** – This is the most common form of depression that can impact anyone based on phenomena (what happens in their life) that can trigger depression. Most people are sad based on different situations; after their loved one dies, the loss of a job, or any tragic event.

- **Comorbidities** – The presence of two of more medical conditions in the same person. For example, a person who is diagnosed with bipolar and schizophrenia is considered to have the presence of comorbidity. People with Schizophrenia are at a greater risk of developing depression.

These types of depressive states can be diagnosed and treated by the right medical professional. Depression is not a death sentence, and your life is not over. Your mood condition can be treated, you just have to seek the consultation of a medical professional to get an accurate diagnosis, so that you can receive the best treatment program for your condition. What works for one person might not work for everyone, so it is best to be accurately diagnosed to ensure that you get the best treatment.

The truth is, no one is 100% sure about what causes depression. Nevertheless, sometimes depression is brought on by certain medication, drug use, or illnesses that change the brain's normal functioning and cause major depressive symptoms. If you experience depression, you should seek treatment to avoid the symptoms worsening.

No one is immune to suffering from some form of depression, no matter how happy or privileged you might be. The only difference is that some people learn how to manage situations that can cause depression, in a much better way. Untreated depression can lead to suicidal thoughts. If you or anyone you know is having suicidal thoughts, please seek help immediately.

The cause of depression is not a one-size fits all approach condition. There are several speculative factors that can cause depression, but not everyone who engages in any of these things listed below will develop depression. The factors are:

- **Abuse** – If you have a past where you experienced any type of abuse, whether as a child or an adult, you may be more likely to experience a major depressive episode that requires you to seek professional treatment.

- **Medication** – There are drugs that are supposed to treat other illnesses that can cause depression, in some individuals. Some of the medications that could increase the risk of developing major depression are: acne drugs, antiviral drugs, and corticosteroids.

- **Conflict** – People who are susceptible to experiencing depressive episodes will develop worse symptoms when there are a lot of conflict situations in their life with family, colleagues, relationships, or friends. Crime victims can also develop depression due to feelings of powerlessness and shame they could experience as a result from being victimized.

- **Loss** – Most people can experience a loss of a relationship, monetary loss, or loss by death and can overcome these things. However, people who have a challenging time coping with a loss might experience some form of depression.

- **Genetics** – Research indicates that mental disorders can be due to genetics. If you have a parent or sibling who has a depressive disorder, you may be three times more likely to develop depression. However, just because someone in your family might suffer from a mental illness does not always mean that you will also suffer from a mental illness. Researchers still do not know the mechanisms behind what triggers depression or the gene that might cause depression.

- **Personal Challenges** – Some people who experience divorce, estranged familial relationships, gender identity challenges, and familial problems that result from being considered an "outcast," because of your sexual preferences can lead to some form of depression, and if not treated the depressive state can become worst. This can sadly happen for people whose sexuality and gender identity are not accepted by loved ones.

- **Serious Illness** – Heart disease, diabetes, cancer, chronic pain, and other serious illnesses can lead to some form of depression. When someone's life changes suddenly due to an illness, it can be hard to cope and accept their new reality *(Fulghum, 2021)*.

- **Substance Abuse** – In regard to substance abuse, it is not always clear what came first: depression, or addiction. Many people believe that substance abusers often are self-medicating to overcome their depressive state or other illnesses. Those who engage in substance abuse usually end up making their situation worse. Drugs and alcohol are depressants. Drugs that include hypnotics, tranquilizers, or sedatives can provoke a stress reaction, panic attack, sleep disorder, and anxiety which can lead to depression. Alcohol slows down brain functioning and neural activity as well and is considered a central nervous system *depressant* (Recovery Ways, 2018).

Keep in mind that it is possible that some people can experience any of these things without suffering from depressive disorders. There are many signs and symptoms of depression. But remember, only a trained medical professional can make an accurate diagnosis. Some of the signs and symptoms to look for are:

- **Irritable Mood** – If you feel easily irritated, all the time, have feelings of excessive sadness, you could be experiencing depression.

- **Overwhelming Sadness** – If you find that you are crying a lot and are sad about everything that is happening in your life, it is a sign that you may have depression.

- **Loss of Interest** – If there are things that you used to love to do and now you cannot find any joy or interest in doing those things, which could be a sign of depression.

- **Weight Changes** – Often, depressed individuals have changes in appetite and either eat too much or eat too little. When you no longer care about what you eat or how much or how little, that could be a sign of depression.

- **Sleep Disturbances** – Many depressed people have a challenging time falling asleep, staying asleep, or sleep all the time, and would prefer to sleep rather than do anything else.

- **Restlessness** – Some depressed people need to constantly move or are unable to calm their mind. They are hyperactive, suffer from anxiety and insomnia.

- **Sluggish and Tired** – Feelings of exhaustion, overwhelmed, and tired. Some people are usually on "autopilot mode," with no enthusiasm or significant effort to accomplish tasks.

- **Worthlessness** – Many depressed people feel unworthy, engage in self-doubt talk, and lack self-efficacy. They usually engage in negative thought that leads them to thinking that no one likes them nor want to be around them, and often question their purpose for living.

- **Guilt Feelings** – Many depressed people experience feelings of guilt. They believe that they are the blame for everything that happens to them, and they often feel shameful.

- **Problems Concentrating** – Depression can make it hard to focus and concentrate on anything. The mind wanders from one thought to the next, which usually leads to being confused about what you were doing or should be focused on.

- **Poor Decision Making** – Many depressed people usually do not make good decisions, because some will try almost anything to make themselves feel better. Doing "anything" is not the best decision. The word, "anything" could mean engaging in substance abuse, excessively shopping, gambling, having an affair, and other negative things to try to mask the depression.

- **Thoughts of Dying** – Some depressed people think about dying a lot. They go to sleep and hope to not wake up, which is one of the reasons that a lot of people who suffer from depression tend to sleep a lot.

- **Thoughts of Suicide** - Not all depressed people experience suicidal ideation. However, many could think about very well-thought-out plans on how they want to carry out the act of suicide *(Leonard, 2022)*.

If you or anyone you know has any of these signs and/or symptoms, please seek immediate professional help. Please take depression very seriously. No, you will not just "snap out of it." No, depression will not just go away without getting the proper help to heal. If you suffer from depression, do not be ashamed, it is more common than most people are willing to admit, and it is treatable. Despite the signs and symptoms that you might experience, there are strategies that could help you get through depression. Those strategies are:

Sleep Control – There are some studies that show that sleep control can help improve depression - specifically sleep deprivation, which we mentioned earlier. This is not a good thing for people with bipolar disorder to do, though. Basically, the way it works is you limit sleep to six or seven hours a night and do not allow yourself to nap or sleep between your specific sleep time.

- **Exercise** – Exercise releases endorphins that make you feel good. You may not feel that great while you are doing it, however, people usually feel better when it is over. Try to at least get out and walk for 20 to 30 minutes a day. You will get the added benefit of more vitamin D, which can also help.

- **Diet** – If you are eating poorly, improving your diet can help. Your brain uses glucose to work. If you are not eating enough vegetables and fruit, you may not be getting enough glucose. Some people on low-carb diets who are not eating vegetables can experience signs of depression.

- **Vitamins** – It is a good idea to ask your doctor to do a blood test to assess vitamin levels. Vitamins like B12 (helps keep your blood and nerve cells healthy), B3 (Niacin helps to lower cholesterol, boost brain function, and ease arthritis), and B6 (helps keep the nervous system and immune system healthy and is good for normal brain development) can be missing from your diet. With any vitamin, make sure that you do not take them in large doses, because they can have an adverse effect. In addition, many people who suffer from depression have vitamin D deficiencies. Vitamin D is good for reducing inflammation and helping to build bone health.

- **Journaling** – It is helpful to write down your thoughts and feelings each day. Make sure that when you are writing down your thoughts, you also write down good thoughts to counteract any negative thought. The brain tends to focus on anything you think about, so if you think about the positives in your life while keeping a gratitude journal, you may find that you feel better. Daily positive affirmations are also good things to write down.

- **Meditation** – Starting to practice meditation can help you in many ways. It's good to try to focus on nothing, except breathing, for a short period of time each day. You can learn about how to meditate by reading books and viewing Meditation videos on YouTube. Meditation can relax your mind and decrease stress and anxiety.

- **Light Therapy** – For some people who have seasonal depression, light therapy can help them feel better. Research states that the key is to do it in the morning before 10 or 11 am, only for about 10 to 15 minutes, and to never do it at night. Some people only need to do it occasionally, but you want to do it prior to the symptoms developing, rather than after they have already started.

- **Reduce Alcohol Consumption** – As I mentioned previously, alcohol is a central nervous system depressant, it slows down brain functioning. So, if you want help dealing with depression, you want to reduce or eliminate your alcohol consumption. Most people who suffer from alcoholism experience mood disorders that could change from mania to manic depression. Marijuana is also both a stimulant that has depressant like effects, as well as psychoactive, and hallucinogenic effects, all of which change a person's brain function and can produce anxiety and feelings of paranoia. Long-term use of marijuana can decrease the number of neurotransmitters released in the brain, making the dopamine levels go down and creating low energy, consistent with the effects of depression. Avoid self-medicating. Get professional help.

- **Do Things You Enjoy** – Even though you do not feel like doing things, the worst thing you can do is isolate yourself and stop doing things that you enjoy. You do not have to be as active as you were, however, try to do something you used to love at least weekly. It'll make you feel a sense of purpose and bring back your joy.

- **Try Something New** – As we age, we change. Maybe, you do not like the things you used to do. Why not find something new to try? You may find a whole new love for something you never considered before. As long as it is safe to do, try it.

- **Talk to People You Trust** – Hopefully, you have some people in your life that you can trust to talk to about what you are going through. You do not have to tell them everything about what is going on in your life, but if you have one person that you can confide in, it can make you feel less alone, more understood, and relieved to not hold onto what is bothering you.

- **Get into Nature** – The best thing anyone can do for their mood and overall health is to get back to nature.

If you live in a city, it can be hard. There are zoos and atriums and other ways to get into nature such as parks. Try to go outside at least once a day for just 20 to 30 minutes.

- **Find Support** – Sometimes, you need support outside of your friends and family. Thankfully, today there are Facebook groups, Meetups.com, and other ways to find support groups for almost any type of cause or purpose. Try out a few different groups, based on the type of help and support you are seeking, so that you can find the right support group for you *(Masley, 2005)*.

These strategies might seem unattainable for some people or might seem like a lot. However, you are worth the time and effort that it will take to help you cope with grief, defeat depression, and get to your other side of through.

The best way to approach self-help is to make goals for yourself that you can accomplish within a short period of time. The more you experience success, the more you will stick to your plan. If you stop your own progress, remember, you can always make a fresh start and try again until you are successful. Keep in mind that tomorrow is not promised, so now is the time to get the help that you need. Don't take any day for granted.

III. Don't Take Any Day for Granted

When we experience something traumatic, it can be difficult to get past the trauma. However, every day that we spend feeling lost and hopeless, is a day of wasted time and energy. Tomorrow is not promised, so do not take any day for granted. Live in the moment. Live in the present. Live in the now. We need to appreciate life and we need to appreciate the people in our life. You never know when it will be the last time that you will see someone, so you must make the best out of each moment you spend with others. Life is unpredictable. We can plan for the future, or at least try. However, know that even our plans might not go the way that we hoped for. You have to get to the point where you know that even when things do not always go the way you think they should, life is still worth living. Try not to waste your time and energy on things that you cannot control.

The unfortunate thing about life is, sometimes, you do not get some moments back (meaning you do not always get the opportunity to redo things). As I began writing this book with Erica, I started to reflect on the moments that I took for granted that I will not get back. When my grandmother, Viola "Mody" Clement passed away, my family and I did not know that her passing would change our lives forever. The dynamics of the family unit changed. We did not see each other as much as we used to see each other. Watching my grandmother grow ill and eventually die was not easy for me, because my grandmother was like a second mother to me. During the time I lived with her I can remember putting hair grease in her hair, brushing her hair a hundred times to help it grow, rubbing Absorbine Jr. on her aching back, going shopping with her, her teaching me how to scale a fish, she would often come to my elementary school to pick up my report card, she shared her coffee with me, and we watched Wheel of Fortune, General Hospital, As the World Turns, and Guiding Light together. I cherished the moments that we spent together, and I miss her dearly. I was young when my grandmother died, and I did not understand much about death or grief at the time of her death. What I did know is that I did not like to see her lose a lot of weight nor see her hair thinning. It was hard for me to watch, so I distanced myself after my mother, sister, and I moved out of my grandmother's house.

I did not visit as often as I should have. I took those days for granted. After she passed away, I realized that those days I did not see her were days that I will never get back. I carried the guilt of that feeling for years. After my grandmother died, I did not want to go back to her house, because there are so many memories in the house that we shared together. It was extremely painful for me to not see her there anymore. At that time, I did not think about how my cousins, who still lived with my grandmother, would feel about me not coming back to see them. I do not even know if anyone else went back to the house to visit my cousins. I was about fourteen, and mentally too young to understand that sometimes other people need to know you care about them too. I took those days for granted and with each passing day, we grew apart. Unfortunately, this happens a lot in families when the elder of the family passes away. I am sure that we were all grieving in our own way.

"Mody" was like a mother to everyone who lived with her. So, I know that all of us felt this great loss. Perhaps, if we were grieving together, the grieving process might have been a little easier for everyone who lived with my grandmother. Unfortunately, we will never get that time back, which is why I am strongly encouraging you and telling you to please **do not take the days for granted.** As an adult now, I realize that I should have visited my grandmother more. Perhaps, it was something that she needed, knowing that her time on earth would end sooner than I think it should have. I wish that she were still alive, so that I can give her back all that she has given me. From this experience, I learned that instead of distancing myself trying to escape from the pain, that it was not about me. I was too young to realize that back then. I encourage people to visit their loved ones, even if it is

difficult for them to watch the person in a sickened state. Perhaps, that person may need to see you and the people around them just need to know that you haven't forgotten about them and maybe...all of you can emotionally support each other. Forgive those who may not be there for you, when he/she is having a challenging time coping with grief as well. Reach out for the support that you need and know that You do not have to go through grief in silence or alone.

Cherish every moment you get to spend with your loved ones. Every day that you get the privilege to wake up, it is truly a blessing to not take for granted. You never know how death will impact you. Try hard to not get stuck in your stage of trauma, so that you can learn how to live each day without taking any second for granted. Remember, time moves forward, even when you do not (mentally,

physically, or emotionally) when you are grieving. Grief is a real feeling. It is a feeling that you cannot escape from. Allow yourself to go through the stages without getting stuck in any stage. Don't let grief rob you of living your life to the fullest. Death is an unfortunate part of life that everyone will face one day. Don't think that your life will go on forever. All of us will eventually die. As long you are still breathing, live without taking any day or person in your life for granted.

    It is so important to know that tomorrow is not promised. You have to live and love today. You deserve that! Everyone enters and exits your life for a reason. You should not take the people in your life for granted. You have to forgive, live, and love, today.

You also must love yourself and not take yourself for granted. Don't waste any moment of your life in a place that does not serve your growth and development. You have to because you should. It is beneficial to your health and well-being. Do not put off doing the things that you want to do with your life, because none of us knows whether or not we will have the time to do it "later." Ask yourself, "If I am going to die tomorrow, what would I do today?" Do not just hold that thought in your head and heart, do what you want to do now. You only get one chance to live the life that you want to live, before it is all over. Don't let your dreams die with you. When our loved ones die, do not die with them. Losing a loved one is not easy, but Live on, your loved one would want you to.

IV. Coping with Grief after the Loss of a Friend

Coping with the loss of a friend can be just as hard as dealing with a breakup from a romantic partner. After you lose a friend, you can experience not only grief and depression, but physical ailments such as: loss of appetite, heartache, insomnia, angina, worry, and other psychological symptoms *(Drevitch, 2021)*. Dependent on how close you are to a friend will determine how you might grieve his/her death or a separation. It seems like the older we get, the harder it is to keep and maintain friendships. There is a popular phrase that says, "Friends can be in your life for a reason, a season, or a lifetime." People that we think will be lifetime friends can often break our hearts and wind up only being around for a brief period of time.

There are several reasons why friendships end: people outgrow each other, we have life changes that occur that can shift priorities and the time that they have to spend with friends can become limited (getting married, having a baby, new job, leaving for college, changing jobs), arguments, jealousy, and physically moving away. Sometimes, we may be in a friendship and accept repetitive bad behavior, because we do not want to lose a friend. Over time, we realize that we deserve to be treated better, so we distance ourselves from friends who continuously mistreat us.

As I was writing this book with Lynnette, I began to reflect on one of my friendships. I had a friend where the friendship started out great, but later evolved into a toxic relationship. My "friend" would treat me mean one day and then treat me nice the next day. We were friends for thirty years. We were working at the same job, and we would spend time together often. I treated her like my sister. When I got married, she expressed to me that she did not like my husband. She felt as though he was not on "my level." She would often go on negative rants about my husband, and I would tell her to back off and keep her opinions to herself. This shifted the dynamics of our friendship. She would try to embarrass me in public by starting arguments when we were around other people. I knew that this was not the kind of friend that deserved to be in my life.

What finally ended our thirty-year friendship, was when she said something insulting to me in front of another friend. I was hurt and stunned. I knew that I had to end what I thought was a friendship. Now, I know that friends do not treat you like you are their enemy. I do not know why her attitude towards me started to change, but it was becoming too painful for me to stay friends with her. At first, I went through a period of grieving after losing her as a friend, and then I realized that I had to do some self-care. As much as I cared for my friend, I had to remove myself from this relationship and not look back. I miss the person she was when we first met (nice). I do not miss the mean person that she evolved into. Sometimes, no matter how painful it is, you have to lose some friendships, especially when your "friend" treats you as if you are their "enemy."

Although, you might experience some grief in the beginning after you lose your friend, you will begin to feel better after you engage in self-care.

Self-care includes:

- Putting Your Needs First

- Getting Adequate Rest
- Eating Nutritional Foods
- Getting Emotional Support
- Developing Self-Efficacy
- Exercising
- Loving Yourself
- Engaging in Relaxation and Meditation

V. Coping with Grief after the Loss of a Family Member

As I co-write this book with Lynnette, I reflect on the loss of both of my parents. My mother, Benita, who died from breast cancer when I was 15 years old. I took her death extremely hard. We were remarkably close, and I was not prepared for her passing. My mother had breast cancer and my parents decided not to tell me. I knew she was not feeling her best, but I had no idea it was cancer. I remember preparing for my eighth-grade graduation, and my mother was in the hospital for a week. I kept asking her if she was going to make it to my graduation, and she kept saying, yes. I really wanted her to be there because I was the Valedictorian of my graduating class. She was discharged from the hospital minutes before my graduation. She did not let wild horses stop her from attending. She died the summer before I started 10th grade. I never thought I would lose my mom so early in life. I learned firsthand that death was final, and I held on to that grief for a long time. I still feel the pain of losing my mother. I still experience anger when thinking about wanting my mother to be here with me. There are days when I want to talk to her and really need her advice, but have to figure things out on my own, because she is no longer here.

After losing my mother when I was fifteen, I lashed out at my father, Ronald. Back then, I was not as close to my father, like I was close to my mother. I was heartbroken and grieving from losing her. I was so hurt and angry, and one day I yelled at my dad telling him that I wished he died instead of my mom. My dad looked me directly into the eyes and yelled back saying he wished I died instead of my mother. I was so hurt. My body was so weak that it felt like I melted into the floor. I was devastated that he said that to me. I did not mean what I said, but it felt like he really meant what he said. I realized that we were both grieving from the loss of my mother. After that argument, I felt more alone and abandoned. I made a promise to myself that I would never speak to my father like that again. It took a few years, but we eventually became remarkably close. Knowing that neither one of us really meant what we said to each other, we forgave one another. My dad was an elderly parent and had me at 51 years old. He died when I was an adult and he lived to be 87 years old. It is important to not mistreat people, because you are hurting.

The death of a parent can affect adult children psychologically and physically.

And, although we understand that the loss of a parent is inevitable, that knowledge does not lessen the grief when a mother or father dies. It can take a long period of time to grieve after losing your parents. Nowadays, most jobs want you to recover from grief quickly and will give you about three days off from work and expect you to return to work and conduct business as usual. Three days may not be enough time. **Grieving** the loss of a parent is unique to each person. There is no timeframe to when the grieving will end. Everyone deals with the loss in their own way.

However, below are some strategies to help you understand that you are not alone in what you might go through in the grieving process.

Let's first discuss what you might feel after losing a parent.

- Lost
- Fear
- Confused
- Relief
- Alone
- Sadness

Now, let's discuss some suggestions on how to support yourself after the death of a parent.

- Talk to someone
- Find ways to remember them
- Plan ahead on what to do on anniversaries

After losing your parents, it will be difficult to figure out a way to do things independently. However, you will learn that despite your circumstances, you will be okay. You will have days when you are okay mentally and emotionally, but there will also be days that you become saddened when thinking about the loss.

As Erica and I are writing this book about coping with grief, I began to cry realizing that I am about to have to minister to myself as well when thinking about the people that I recently lost. In 2021, I lost my little cousin, Rashede Clement Jr., to senseless gun violence, and two of my friends, Stacey Florio, and Dr. Renee Reynolds-Lawson, who passed after complications from Covid-19. Losing loved ones is not easy and helping people cope with a loss is not easy. May they all rest in peace. I realize that helping people cope with grief is not easy, because everyone copes with grief in different ways. It can be difficult to tell a mother and father how to cope after the loss of their children. It can be difficult to tell a child how to cope after the loss of their parents, or to tell a spouse how to cope after the loss of their spouse. There is no one size fits all approach to coping with grief. However, this book is written with the intent to help you figure out what works best for you, while giving you some strategies that you might find useful as you go through the grieving process.

Allow yourself to go through the stages of grief, just do not get stuck in sadness and depressive state forever. I cannot restate this enough, Try not to get stuck at the stage where the trauma occurred. I know that it is not always easy to deal with grief, so the goal of this book is to inspire you, encourage you, and give you hope in knowing that you can overcome the sadness of grief and find your happiness again, if you really try to positively overcome grief and don't let the grief overtake you.

VI. Coping with Grief After the Loss of a Relationship

Most people do not realize that after the loss of a relationship, people can go through the same stages of grief as if the person died. A loss is an absence of someone's presence, which is similar to a death. Whether you are in a boyfriend/girlfriend relationship or a marriage, the pain from the loss can be quite difficult to manage. When a relationship ends, allow yourself the time you need to heal before moving on to your next relationship. Losing a boyfriend/girlfriend might not be as traumatic as losing a spouse. However, it is still a loss that can cause you to experience grief.

The loss of a marriage can be devastating. Marriage is not for the faint of heart. In a marriage, there has to be compromise and sacrifices made. Some people want to rush into marriage and then they are surprised when the marriage does not work out. Two people grow together and develop a strong bond, so the absence of either party, can be quite devastating. The loss of the marriage is not easy, especially if divorce is on the horizon. It surprises me that many partners feel embarrassed when they consider divorcing their spouse. Statistics show that about 50% of all marriages end in divorce. It is not something that anyone should be ashamed or embarrassed about if their marriage ends. We should not feel like a failure, when a marriage or relationship ends in divorce or separation.

People who experience the loss of a marriage might experience similar feelings, as if the person has died. They might feel alone, unloved, have physical symptoms, problems sleeping, loss of appetite, experience mood swings, have thoughts of suicide, feel like a failure, engage in substance abuse and/or promiscuity, and feel rejected. It is important that you know that the loss is not always your fault. In the midst of going through any type of loss, it can be devastating. According to Kara Hartzell of *Hartzell Counseling and Therapy*, some of the ways to cope with grief after the loss of a spouse are (whether by death or divorce):

- Practice Self Compassion
- Understand there is a Grief Process
- Lean On Your Friends for Support
- Allow Yourself to Let Go

- Maintain Healthy Boundaries with your Ex (if divorced or separated)
- Commit to Rediscovering Yourself
- Seek Grief Therapy

Some other suggestions are:

- Limit or Avoid Escape Behaviors
- Honor Your Deceased Spouse
- Do Things When They Feel Right to You
- Stay Open to Experiencing Happiness
- Maintain Some Structure in Your Life

Dealing with grief is never an easy process. However, it is a process that everyone must go through at some point.

If you lose a spouse to separation and you have children together, you will have to find a way to communicate with each other, so that you can be good co-parents for the sake of the children.

You can experience grief in relationships, even if death is not the cause of grief. A breakup of the relationship can cause you to experience grief. Most people try to make their relationship work successfully. One of the number one reasons why relationships break up, is the result of not knowing how to effectively communicate with one another. When couples do not know how to communicate, they tend to argue. Sometimes, people want to be right and win an argument rather than just conceding to make the other partner happy. It is not about losing yourself to concede to what someone else wants, even if it makes you unhappy. It is not about always being right or wrong, it is about finding a compromise, so that both of you can win and both of you can be happy. Too often, we can get "stuck in our ways," without realizing that a relationship is about two people, so we have to be comfortable with not always getting everything that we want. We have to learn how to embrace change, if we truly want to heal.

VII. Embracing Change

When there are things that change in our lives, we do not always approach those changes with optimism. Most of us like to feel comfortable, and change makes us feel uncomfortable. A lot of elders have a challenging time embracing change. For example, if they have been doing a certain thing for years, it will be difficult to get them to try to do things differently. Younger people can also have challenges with adapting to change, because they might get used to a routine, and when the routine changes it could take a while to get adjusted to doing something different.

However, all of us need to be flexible enough to adapt to the changes we encounter in life. Just like death, change is inevitable. It is unpredictable to know in advance what we will encounter in life that will cause us to have to adjust and adapt (change). The inability to adapt to new environments and new situations will impact your happiness. It will impact your happiness, if you do not know how to cope with whatever it is that is causing you to be sad.

    Just like grief, embracing change is a process. We must first acknowledge and accept what needs to change or what has changed. Then, we must think about how we will be impacted by the change and formulate a strategic plan on how we will adapt to the change processes. In the beginning, we might have to modify the plan, especially if we are resistant to change. Keep in mind that it is not going to kill you to try doing something different, so try to do something different. Especially, if it is in your best interest and well-being. If feeling sad and depressed is not the mental state or mood that you want to remain in, engage in positive activities to change your mood.

Coping with challenges is not always easy and is not a one-sided approach to overcoming the challenges. You have to figure out what works best for you. Figuring out the formula that works is not easy. Many people will tell you what helped them get through life challenges, including Erica and I, however, you have to find what works for you.

The formula for what works is usually based on what makes You happy; what You enjoy doing, and what is the least complicated thing to do that You can do consistently. Coping with grief will make you have to work towards getting through the stages consistently, so that you do not get stuck at any stage. Overcoming grief is a progressive continuum that can seem never-ending. However, as each day passes, you will begin to learn how to cope with grief in a better way, and you might even be able to help coach someone else through the grieving process as well.

VIII. How to Help Your Loved One Cope With Grief?

Helping your loved one cope with grief is not easy. However, they might lean on you for comfort and support. It is important to be empathetic, compassion, sympathetic, and a great listener. Refrain from telling people how to feel and when they should stop grieving. It is also important that you do not lose yourself in the process of trying to help others. When you are always there for other people, it can begin to affect your mental health.

Find a balance where you take time for yourself and practice self-face without feeling like you are being selfish. Self-care is not selfish. It can sometimes get mentally draining to deal with your own personal problems, while helping others cope with theirs. Setting boundaries is critical to your own well-being. It is okay to be there for others when they need you, just as much as it is okay to be there for you, when you need you. It is also okay to refer them to get professional help, especially if they begin to isolate themselves. Sometimes, people isolate themselves from others, when they are dealing with grief. It is okay to give them some time to grieve on their own. However, let them know that you are there for them when they need you. Make sure you check-in to ask how they are doing?

One of the first things that people do when they feel sad or depressed is isolate themselves. Sometimes, you distance yourself when you know that someone is sick, suffering or dying, to protect yourself from feeling emotional or depressed. However, the person that is sick, suffering or dying really needs to know that you love and care about them and he/she might want to see you one last time. However, there are others who do not want people to see them in a certain health state. You have to respect what he/she wants, while at the same time being supportive of your own needs as well. We have to be mindful of the fact that everyone goes through the stages of grief in their own way and at their own pace.

It can be difficult for some people to let go of their loved one, because they might tell themselves, "I'll have nothing left to hold onto, if I let him/her go." However, sometimes, letting go helps you hold on to YOU and your emotional sanity. Nevertheless, never make an emotional decision in a quick moment that you might later regret. Take the time you need to think things through. Even if other people try to tell you what they think you should do, you have to do what works best for you.

We can offer advice on how someone can cope with grief in a better way. However, there are some things in life that you cannot coach people through, if they are not ready or willing to listen. Nevertheless, if you are ready and willing to listen, everybody is coachable.

Never tell someone when they should stop grieving. Telling someone when they should stop grieving is telling them that they are not entitled to feel their real emotions. Before you judge anybody whom you feel has been grieving "for too long," learn about their life story, so you can understand what makes him/her think and behave the way they do. Know that everyone is not like you.

Some of the things that you can do to help people cope with grief are:

- Encourage them to engage in positive mental "escapes." It is okay to engage in Positive mental escapes and not negative escapes, like drug use, drinking, overeating, and sexual promiscuity. When you come down from the high, the trauma is still there, which is what makes engaging in negative behaviors habitual.

- Seeking Spiritual counseling is one of the best ways to help people cope with grief. However, if you are not spiritual, you too can still overcome grief with a good support system and/or good mental health practices like meditation, positive affirmations, and reading daily devotionals. When you experience traumatic situations, it is important to not get mad at God...sometimes that is easier said than done.

- Pay attention to your mental health and well-being, as well as others. Get the help and support you need so that you do not lose your sanity.

- **Listen** – When someone who is depressed is venting to you, just listen. You do not need to give them advice on how to fix their problem unless they ask for it. Let them talk; show them that you are listening by paraphrasing back to them what they have said or by looking them in the eyes or kindly touching their hand or shoulder, if it is age appropriate.
- **Show You Care** – It is okay to show emotion when someone is emotional around you or is demonstrating dangerous symptoms of depression. Sometimes you may have to show them that you care by calling in a professional if your friend is suicidal. Be willing to receive their emotions and expressions that they might "hate you" in the moment of trying to get them help.

However, get them the help they need anyway.

- **Don't Criticize** – The worst thing you can do is criticize someone who is depressed. Most likely, they already have low self-worth. This is not the time for tough love or that type of honesty. Just be there for them without judgment.
- **Don't Give Ultimatums** – It might be tempting, especially when it is a spouse or a child, to threaten and give ultimatums. But, doing so could make things worse. People who suffer from depression do not make good decisions, so they are not going to do what you want just because they are going to lose you. In fact, they are more likely to push you away.
- **Understand That Their Pain is Real** – Depression sufferers are no different from anyone suffering from

another disease such as diabetes or cancer. Their pain is real. Their feelings are real. They cannot just stop depression instantaneously. If they could, they would.

- **Do Not Give Advice** – Sometimes, when you give unsolicited advice, the response is usually defensive. Remember, you are not an experienced therapist, so keep your advice to yourself about what to do about depression. It is good that you want to help, but when someone is depressed, their mental state could require professional help. While some things might work well such as exercise, eating right, and so forth, instead of telling someone what they should do, invite them to do things with you that they might enjoy.
- **Don't Say That You Understand** – Even if you have suffered from

depression yourself, you do not know how they personally feel, so do not say that you do. Most of the time, we think we are helping and empathizing with them when we say that we understand how they feel. However, sometimes people who experience depression can be difficult to connect with on an emotional level. Everyone has different methods of coping, and they might view your expressed empathy as being self-centered. Don't turn things around to be about you, because they're not going to be ready to accept your help until they're in therapy.

- **Educate Yourself on Depression** – Read books and watch documentaries about depression to help you learn about what depression is, so that you become aware of the danger signs and can get the help you need.

If you fear that your loved one will harm themselves or others, ensure them that you have the number to call at your fingertips to get them help from a professional. If you have friends or family members who are suffering from depression as a result from grief, there are ways that you can help them without feeling as if you are walking on eggshells. Depression is a horrible illness that can be fatal if left untreated. Hopefully, when you understand that no one wants to be depressed and that they cannot just fix it on their own, you will find it easier to be supportive. Let them know that it is okay to go through to get through.

IX. How to Help a Child Understand Grief and Loss

Most of the strategies in this book about coping with grief are applicable to people that are at an appropriate age where they understand what loss and grief are. So, we decided that it could be beneficial to also help you to help your child understand what grief and loss is from a childlike perspective.

Grief and loss also impact children. Sometimes, children do not want to express how they feel or might not even know what it is that they are feeling. When you talk to your child about grief and loss, explain the difference between the two. Let him/her know that loss is something that could potentially happen again, but there is no guarantee that anything that you lose will return, similar to the loss of a job, a friend, or a divorce. Grief is something more permanent and usually occurs after a death or some other traumatic experience.

Dependent on the age of the child, most children do not usually understand what it means to grieve, nor what it means when someone dies. It can be challenging to know how to approach those situations when children begin to ask questions about not seeing someone anymore. Your response to the question of what happened, why, and will I ever see them again, should always be age appropriate. Some of the ways that you can respond to those questions are:

- Listen and comfort them, use simple words and comparisons

to describe what it means when someone dies.

- Be prepared for the child to respond emotionally and expect that they will have more questions.
- Reassure the child that it is not their fault.
- Express that it is okay to cry or feel sad, as well as to talk openly about how you feel. Reassure them that they can come talk to you about anything when they need to talk.
- Do not lie to the child about what happened.
- Work with them to come up with a way to memorialize the deceased.

- Show them love and compassion.

Each child will react to death in a different way. Pay attention to how your child reacts after any type of loss and get him/her the help that they need. It is okay to sit the child down and be empathetic and honest with them, letting them know that you have sad news that you want to share with them. Then, tell them honestly what happened (i.e., Dad and I decided to get a divorce, which means that we will be living apart and you will not see him every day like you're used to. We will be moving. We still love you and will continue to do the best co-parenting that we can do to make sure that the both of us are still in your life, and our decision is not your fault; or your grandmother died today and that means that her body organs stopped working and we will not see her again, but we can go visit her grave site anytime you would like. Then, ask your child if they have any questions and how they feel after hearing the news. If they have questions, answer their questions with care, empathy, love, and give them a hug and let them know that everything will be okay.

Do not withhold information from your child, thinking that you are protecting them. When you withhold information from your child and they later find out that information from someone else, they will usually resent you for not telling them. You do not have to disclose all of the details about what happened, but at least let your child know the end result of what happened. Try to maintain the same structure and routine as much as possible, so that the child can still feel like they are still living a "regular" life.

If your child is struggling to overcome grief, seek out the help of a counseling professional. Just like an adult, let the child know that it is okay to go through to get through.

X. Go Through to Get Through

In life we go through ups and downs, and death for most people is one of the downsides of life (dependent on how you view death). Death is an inevitable part of life. As you go through life, keep God at the center of your life and God will get you through anything. If you are not a spiritual person, it could be more difficult to learn how to cope with life's challenges. Because of your lack of faith and not believing in the power of God, it could be easier for you to become hopeless and struggle through the stages of grief. What helped me through the stages of grief after losing my grandmother, "Mody," was knowing that she would want me to be healthy and happy, knowing that she was no longer suffering or in pain, and knowing that she and God are always with me in spirit, as well as believing that God will help me heal. There was a time when I did not forgive myself for not visiting my grandmother as often as I should have after we moved out and I wished that I could get that time back. However, I had to forgive myself, knowing that I was young and did not know what I was doing or how it could impact anyone else. I had to forgive myself, so that I could heal.

    Forgiving yourself is a process, just like coping with grief is a process. I truly wish that she were alive today, so that I can give her back everything that she has given me, so that I can thank her for her sacrifices, give her everything that she deserves, and so that she can be proud of the woman that I am now. I would not be telling the truth if I said that I did not miss her and that I still cry when I think about her. Yes, I allow myself to feel. I allow myself to be human. I allow myself to express emotions. However, I no longer get stuck in those feelings or emotions. I cherish the memories, live in the present, and move on and live for today. There is no easy way to deal with grief. You have to go through the stages of grief, to get to the other side of grief, which is healing. Yes, the other side of grief leads to healing.

Healing is a much better place to be. No one likes the feeling of depression or sadness. However, everyone who heals likes how it feels to be healed. Even if you get sad sometimes or even cry sometimes, it does not mean that you are not healed. It means that you are human. If you are sad all the time and you cry all the time, that means you are not healed, and you could be stuck at your stage of trauma. I want to encourage you that with each passing day, if you allow yourself to go through the stages of grief and work towards your healing, you will feel better, you will learn how to cope with grief, you will learn how to laugh again, you will learn how to love again, and you will learn how to continue living. Despite which type of loss you encounter that causes you to experience grief, whether it is the loss of a job, the loss of financial stability, the loss of good health due to illness, the loss of a child, the loss of a family member, a pet, a friendship, a relationship, a divorce, etc., you can still heal.

When you experience any type of loss, at the onset of the loss, it is not always easy to accept. To overcome the loss, you first have to get through the denial stage of grief and Accept that what occurred is real. The loss might change your life forever, however, staying stuck in the stage of denial will also change your life forever. It is a matter of whether or not you want to change your mindset to positive or negative. You can control your thoughts and emotions, but it is something that you have to master, because it is not always easy. For some, it might seem easier to stay stuck in denial, because doing so does not require the "work" and conscious effort that it will take to get unstuck. You have to be willing to go through an extremely vulnerable and open emotional state of mind to get to your other side of through. Allow yourself to feel. It is okay to let go of the physical person and know that they will forever be with you in spirit. Always remember, your loved one wants you to be happy and whole.

    I want you to know that it is okay to grieve. Some people do not give themselves the proper time they need to grieve. Those people might feel that experiencing grief is a sign of weakness and they try to be stronger. If you do not allow yourself to go through the stages of grief, your body will naturally go through the stages without your permission. You will either cry, overindulge in negative behaviors, or overwork yourself to try to keep your mind off what you are feeling. If you hold in your emotions for an extended period, it could lead to major health problems, like a stroke or heart attack, or even a nervous breakdown.

Allow yourself to go through the stages of grief properly, so that you can get to your other side of through. Life does get better…. How you feel right now, will get better. Don't wait to love. Do not wait to live. Don't wait to pursue your dreams. Do not focus so much on the loss that you cannot appreciate the blessings that you have right now. Don't waste time thinking about all the reasons why your plan will not work. Focus your energy on taking the necessary steps to create the best life for yourself that you can possibly make.

Despite what causes you to feel grief, you can cope with grief in a better way. Death is not the only reason people experience grief. The people who are not the victims of crimes, but have witnessed the crimes can also experience grief, even if they did not lose a loved one. When you have empathy and compassion for others, even if you are not directly affected by a loss or other traumatic experience, you feel compassion for those who are struggling with grief and loss. Going through the stages of grief is not a sign of weakness, it is a sign of strength. It takes strength to be able to deal with what you are experiencing emotionally. There are important things that you need to be mindful of when you are trying to overcome grief. Those things are:

- I cannot reiterate enough the importance of paying attention to your mental health and well-being. Your peace of mind is important.

- Make sure that you are getting the help you need, it is important. Getting help does not mean that something is wrong with you.

- Don't isolate yourself or other people. Let people in who are trying to help and not hinder you and want the best for you.

- Remember that You are important, and You matter. Try not to get so caught up in Your pain and grief that You forget about You. Don't forget about loving You. Do not forget about taking care of You.

- Never forget about You and Your happiness.

Go through the stages of grief, so you can get to your happiness. Your happiness is in your healing.

XI. Your Happiness is in Your Healing

One of the main goals in life is to be happy. Happiness is an emotional state of mind that creates positive thinking, a positive mood, and feeling good about oneself, and about life. The challenging part about happiness is that it is an emotion/feeling that can sometimes fluctuate from happiness to sadness, if we allow our emotions to control us. It is so important to be able to control your emotional state of mind, because your mind controls your body.

What impacts your emotions, impacts your body, and your health is important to your well-being. When you can control your mind, you can control your mood, as well as your behaviors.

Our life experiences can create feelings of happiness and sadness, depending upon the situations we encounter. When dealing with grief and loss, your happiness depends on how long you allow your mind to remain in a state of depression, hopelessness, and defeat. Too often, people dealing with grief get stuck at the stage where the trauma occurred. It is not easy to coach someone through the grieving process, because each of us has our own way of dealing with life events.

When you are trying to cope with grief, keep in mind that your loved one would not want you to "die" with them. Live on and take their memory and spirit with you forever.

This book is designed to encourage you to think about how your loved one would want you to continue to live a happy and healthy lifestyle, with or without them. It is written with the purpose of helping you cope with grief.

Before we encourage you to cope with grief in a better way, we had to share our own personal stories about coping with grief. Although, our loved ones have been deceased for a long time, we still remember them and sometimes cry when thinking about them. However, as time goes by, we learned how to cope with grief and not let grief consume us or prevent us from living and being happy. When something good happens to us, we tend to be happy and when something bad happens to us, we tend to be sad.

Therefore, it is better to have joy, because in spite of what happens, joy is constant. You can achieve joy by healing from whatever is causing your sadness. To do so, YOU must be honest with yourself about what is causing your sadness. If you are sad, ask yourself right now, "What is causing my sadness?" After you answer that question honestly, ask yourself, "What am I going to do about it, so that I can be happy?" Then, take the necessary steps to work towards being happy. YOU control your happiness.

In life, there are things within our ability to control and there are things that we cannot control. We cannot predict what will happen in our lives, we can only hope for the best. Life is so unpredictable; one day you can have everything that you want in life and the next day, it can all be taken away from you. Nevertheless, we have to continue to work through the trauma and move forward. After a traumatic experience, working through it and moving forward is not always easy.

However, it is important to your mental stability and growth. You have the ability to control how you think and react to every situation in your life. When you are stuck in the stages of grief, that fact might be difficult to understand or accept. However, you have to learn how to control your mind.

One way to control your mind is to practice mindfulness and meditation. Train your brain to think about positive things instead of focusing on negative things. Instead of focusing on the problem, focus on the solution to the problem. Too often, we dwell on our problems, instead of coming up with a solution for the problem.

The more we think about the problem, the more the problem controls our emotional state of mind. When we focus more on how to resolve the problem and work towards the resolution to the problem, our emotional state of mind is usually more optimistic.

Because life is so unpredictable, you have to learn how to handle good and bad situations. Dealing with grief is one of those situations. Life is both good AND bad; we do not get to choose which one we will experience more than the other. However, what we do get to choose is our perspective and how to handle both situations (good and bad). Good things can be the result from bad situations, depending upon how we handle the situation. Have you ever lost a "friend" who always told you what you cannot do, and you thought you needed that friend in your life, but when you stopped hanging around him/her, you realize that you are better off without him/her?

This is one of those situations that you might have viewed as bad, until you realized that it worked out for your good. Too often, we look for others to make us happy. If you are looking for something or someone else to make you happy, you will always be in search of happiness. When you realize and accept that happiness is an inside job, you will learn to search within yourself for happiness.

When we are not happy within, we cannot appreciate the contribution of others who might try to contribute to our happiness, because again...happiness is an inside job. We cannot always predict what will make us happy. No, you cannot predict everything, but you can predict when YOU decide to be happy.

Although you might not clearly see your way to the path of happiness, when you are trying to cope with grief, happiness is always a possibility. However, until you are ready to deal with the emotions that you are feeling in an honest way, you will remain in a depressive, stagnant state. Grieving is a process that you must go through to get through. One of the ways to deal with your emotions and what you are feeling is to be honest about what you are feeling. You also must focus on doing positive things, instead of doing negative things. Engaging in Negative things can get you in trouble and keep you in a depressive state. Stay positive and choose to be HAPPY. Your happiness is in your healing.

There is life after a traumatic experience. There is hope and healing on the other side of your through, and no matter how hard it might be today for you to cope with grief, there is joy on the other side. You can find your joy again. Do the work to go through the grieving process, even though it might be uncomfortable to do. We are praying for your healing. There is happiness in your healing!

If you are having a challenging time coping with grief, below are some additional positive strategies that could help you:

- Acknowledge the pain and sadness that you are feeling and engage in doing positive activities that you enjoy, to ease your mind. Do not try to ignore the pain.

- Do not isolate yourself, spend time with your friends and family doing things that you safely enjoy.

- Seek out professional support services through your church, counseling services, and/or behavioral health facilities. Don't be afraid or embarrassed to talk about what you are experiencing.

- Take care of your physical, emotional, and spiritual health by eating a well-balanced diet, exercise, take time out for you, get adequate rest, and mentally decompress.

- Avoid engaging in self-sabotaging behavior. Avoid sexual promiscuity, drugs, and alcohol abuse. Deal with the real problem in a positive way.

- Take the time you need to heal. Don't interact with hurt people who hurt people.

- Cherish the memories and continue to live in the present.

- Talk to trusted family members and friends about what you are going through and get the professional help that you need.

- Value yourself and your life enough to live on, despite what you are feeling.

- Know that there is no specific time limit for grieving. Just do not get stuck in any of the stages of grief and know that there is a difference between grief and depression.

- When you are sad or depressed, for an extended period of time, seek professional help based on what you are feeling.

- Get involved in a support group related to your type of loss.

- Get involved in a Bible based church and seek spiritual counseling based on your type of loss.

- Seek help from a professional who specializes in Cognitive Behavioral Therapy.

- Engage in self-care and allow yourself time to take care of you.

- Listen to positive affirmations daily, to focus your mind on positive things shifting from the negative.

- If the loss is by death, talk to your loved one in spirit, visit their grave site, show him/her that you are going to be okay and that you will live on in honor of them.

- Understand that it is not your fault.

- Start a journal to write out your feelings and develop strategies to cope in a positive way with grief.

- Seek God's strength, presence, and pray for healing.

- If you are interested in learning how to help a grieving family member or friend, purchase this book for them to read and remind them that you are there to support them through this time, if they need to talk.

- Know that grieving is not easy, and it is an uncomfortable emotion to experience. It is a process that takes time to learn how to cope with grief. It is okay to feel, because you are human. Know that you are not crazy, you are not stupid, you are not weak, you are not a misfit, you are not a problem, you are not a burden, you are not an embarrassment, you are not what you have been through, and you are not alone. You matter, so please get the help that you need to cope better with grief and loss.

We hope that you will apply these suggested strategies that we included in this self-help book, Coping with Grief: Your Happiness is in Your Healing, to help you cope with grief. Below are some additional resources for counseling and support services that can also help you cope as you go through the grieving process. Keep in mind that there is no one-size fits all approach to coping with grief, so allow yourself grace. The best help for coping with grief is usually guided by the instructions from a mental health professional.

We want you to feel whole again. We want you to be happy again. We want you to live again. Do not expect to heal overnight. You could find yourself in the lengthy process of healing. Despite the length of time that it takes you to heal, YOU can overcome grief and regain control over your life and your happiness. If you got to this part of the book, it is because you really want to heal. We are proud of you for taking a step towards healing. Start now on your journey towards healing. Remember, Your Happiness is in Your Healing!

"H.E.A.L.I.N.G. (HEAL, EVEN when ALL things LOOK IMPOSSIBLE, NEVER GIVE UP)." – **Lynnette & Erica**

Resources:

SAMHSA's helps with Anxiety, Depression, Alcohol abuse and Drug abuse – 1-800-662-4357.

RAINN helps with Sexual Abuse – 1-800-656-4673.

Loss of a Job – www.helpguide.org

Grief and Loss Counseling – www.betterhelp.com

Cognitive Behavioral Therapist for Teens and Youth – 1-866-600-9578.

Loss of a spouse or significant other – www.griefconnection.org

Center for Family Services provides counseling for the loss of a Family member, pet, or Friend – 1-877-922-2377.

National Center for Missing and Exploited Children helps with the loss of a Missing Person – 1-800-843-5678.

NAMI provides Mental Health Counseling – 1-800-950-6264.

Resources Continued

The MISS Foundation helps with the loss of a Child – 1-602-279-6477.

Unite, Inc. helps with the loss of a Baby/Miscarriage – 484-758-0002.

National Suicide Prevention Lifeline – 1-800-273-8255 or text 988.

This self-help book, Coping with Grief: Your Happiness is in Your Healing, is written in memory of Viola G. Clement, Dorothy Adams, Denise Clement, David Clement, Jr., Nathaniel Holmes, Sr., Rashede Clement, Jr., Stacey Florio, Renee Reynolds-Lawson, Benita Sterling, Ronald Sterling, Ruby Copes, Helen Walker, Ruby Washington, Brenwanda "Brennie" Smith, Lucious Pleas, and everyone else we lost. May all of them rest well in paradise.

Special thank you to everyone who inspired us to continue to write and bring this creative vision to light! Thank God for blessing us with creative gifts to share with the world! Thank you, Mom, Darlene, and Sister, Danette, for your love and support! Thank you to my co-author, Erica, for working so hard with me to complete this important book! Lynnette's books are available now at most online book retailers.

Rest well mom, Benita, and dad, Ronald. Thank you to everyone who played a part in shaping our thoughts when writing this book! Healing is a process. We wrote this book to help you heal too.

References

Drevitch, G. (2021). Coping With the Loss of a Friendship. *Psychology Today.* Retrieved from: https://www.psychologytoday.com/us/blog/frazzlebrain/202111/coping-the-loss-friendship-0.

Fulghum-Bruce, D. (2021) Causes of Depression. *WebMD*. Retrieved from: https://www.webmd.com/depression/guide/causes-depression.

Hartzell, K. (2021). *Hartzell Counseling & Therapy*. Retrieved from: https://hartzellcounseling.com/how-to-start-rediscovering-yourself-and-healing-after-divorce/.

Kubler-Ross, E., Kessler, D. (2007). On Grief and Grieving: Finding the Meaning of Grief Through the Five Stages of Loss. *Scribner.*

Leonard, J. (2022). Recognizing the Hidden Signs of Depression. *Medical News Today.* Retrieved from:

https://www.medicalnewstoday.com/articles/325513.

Masley, J. (2005). The Role of Exercise, Nutrition, and Sleep in Battle Against Depression. *Family Health Psychiatric & Counseling Center, Pc).* Retrieved from: https://www.fhpcc.com/the-role-of-exercise-nutrition-and-sleep-in-the-battle-against-depression.

Merriam-Webster Dictionary. Grief. Retrieved from:

https://www.merriam-webster.com

Raypole, C. (2022). The Grief of Losing a Parent Is Complex – Here's How to Start Navigating It. *Heathline.com*. Retrieved from:

https://www.healthline.com/health/losing-a-parent.

Recovery Ways. (2018). What Comes First, Depression or Addiction? Retrieved from: https://www.recoveryways.com/rehab-blog/what-comes-first-depression-or-addiction/.

Printed in April 2023
by Rotomail Italia S.p.A., Vignate (MI) - Italy